As We Refer to our Bodies
DARREN C. DEMAREE

8TH HOUSE PUBLISHING
www.8thHousePublishing.com

8th House Publishing
Montreal, Canada

Copyright © 2013 Darren C. Demaree
First Edition

Cover Design © 2013 8th House Publishing

Set in *Caslon* and *Century Gothic*

A CIP catalogue record for this book is available from
LIBRARY AND ARCHIVES CANADA
CATALOGUING IN PUBLICATION
As We Refer to our Bodies / Demaree, Darren C. (1981-)

ISBN 978-1-926716-16-9

8th House Publishing
Montreal, Canada

With special thanks to David Schloss,
Christopher Michel, and Ryan Hilborn
all of whom helped select and edit different
versions of this book.

As We Refer
to Our Bodies

DIRECTIONS FOR LEAVING   5

OHIOS   19

BLACK & WHITE PICTURES   57

Directions For Leaving

Darren C. Demaree

SECRET ANIMAL
for Ben Rathkamp

Let there be
an un-hunching
of the Northwest;

This branch
is for the birds:
the light birds,

the heavy birds
too. Secret
animal, there is
a constant wind

from the bay.
Be sure enough
to jump up into
it, and fly away

when it kicks up.
Do not fear the
water, if it turns.

THE BLIND LIMITS
OF A LIMITED SUGGESTION

It's the glitter
& roll

that suspends
the fine seam

of the curtain:
A sparrow still

sings.
Listen close,

this song
is about one

open window
quickly closing.

THE WHEAT SANK RIPE

The plot allows failure
& as my father moved
through the fields

he did not own, the village
life overcame his urgency,
born of money, the road

to it, he became a legend
of no light, the blackbird
gave context to his shoulder.

TIP OF WHISKEY

I trip on the whiskey
I banged my head
on the whiskey
at the top of the stairs
slammed stars against
& with the whiskey
felt the she in her
best woman parts
with the whiskey
cried whiskey
more whiskey
with the whiskey
& cried whiskey
when everything went

JOY #4

Full flanks
in your hands,

the casual weight
of your

touch takes
the shadows

from the mountain
& ushers them

to the sea
(which is pretty far

from Ohio). Lady,
all of that sun

is ours alone

& your drag
has given us the time

to measure
the lakes our hands

make, with each
stroke of skin.

IMAGINING WINGS

I want to love
the woman on the cliff,
hide my knee caps
in the hem of her skirt,
let her lick the back
of my legs, and, when
we find our breath,
have her pour the wine
over our pressed lips,
keeping the stories
of the town below
the ridge silent.
She would thumb
my Adam's apple
never questioning
our backwards steps,
our terrific leaning,
our last flight.

Darren C. Demaree

KNOX COUNTY FAIR

She asked me to put her in a headlock,
her tensed lips straining for air, naked
ass arched towards the fluorescent lights
of the tent—we, like barnyard animals,
desperate, bent over bricks of straw,
her mouth digging into the soft part
above my elbow, the dirty tears streaming
down my forearms, cries for a transformation
that she could touch, something past I-71,
dreams of a place with satin sashes instead
of cotton, something stronger than my arms,
a life that could knock her breath out
& sustain her body in a constant motion.

WAYS YOU CAN LOSE YOUR HEART #16

For some time, for good
& with so much violence,
could it even be called a fading?
She, in her turn, suffered most.

Me, in my turn, suffered more.
There was a sky where the stars had died
& each time we replaced one

the heat of falling rock would consume
us. I don't remember the colors.
I don't remember the weight of it.
I remember the burning, mostly.

JOY #27

Above the sand,
three floors up
from the turtles,
Emily does the dishes
in a sheer tank-top,
Emily wraps up
the guacamole,
dipping her finger in
one more time
to taste the avocado.

THE SMELL OF A QUIET CITY

This time we just sank
into the junk,
let our arms feel the muck,

the smell of two dirty people,
feigning, racing
to give up first. There

was nothing good
about us then,
but we gained some substance

after, some real hate
for our time together
& that is worth remembering,

that is how, when lit,
bad love scurries
to be warm, in the dark again.

Darren C. Demaree

SHE PAINTS WITH NO FRAME
For Aubrey Hirsch

I like your kind of breaking,
the particle of it, the magic
& the lack of lid on it, the char

that drops blue as truth,
wrapping the physics
of our human restraint

around the infinitely rich
imagination of believers.
I believe in color, I believe

in the suffocation of dark,
I believe that dawn is a flash
of element, human, fantastic,

colliding in Pittsburgh,
with the light touch of before
the reaction made all of us.

OHIOS

Finally, sex like a burned
corn field, raw & rough
& in the dirt, a story peppered
with the word "soiled."

This is something I can tell
friends & family about,
something they will understand:
the land, the flesh,

the blood, the whiskey
before the blue jeans
came off; mild air, so perfect
at all the wrong times.

I remember liking it,
the sudden lightness, how
you slowly ate at me,

nibbled my hamstrings, then
ran to the back of the room.

It took me twenty-nine days
to fall down. When I woke up,
there was a beautiful woman

in the corner, tucking her
shoe over her ankle. Ohio,
coy mistress, now I limp

with the memory of you.

Rust & mist & no
kept promises,
no pennies sewn
into the hemline
of this year,

everybody envies
lilies: their little
moans of beauty
have escaped into
the waters & floated

& floated away.

The sun is up. The sun is gone.
The red barn is still there,

chasing what moves towards it.
Too much of the what is spent

on the silhouette of its coming.
A religion for any moment, I believe

in nothing, I believe in Ohio.
How glad I am to be so simple

as to write love poems for a state
shaped like a swollen heart.

Something, a pace-setter,
a featherless bird too naked
to capture, has flown kamikaze

through your life & is
resting now only because
you've closed your eyes.

Something opened its eyes when
you first did, nestled itself
next to you, in your crib & for

the rest of time will be nose-
to-nose with you, never yielding.

It's amazing
how cavernous
the facial

lacerations become.
I am not ugly.
I am just here.

You & the resultant limbo
(I'm sorry about that too)
falling from our chins,
I have walked far enough.

I am willing to live forever
(I'm sorry about that too)
singing bringing tarnish, green
with hope, blue with hope.

Unlock this door, take on
flesh, pick the strawberry
of this moment for its color:
(I'm sorry about that too).

Some mornings I wake up
fabricated, choosing
the wild lines, elbows
to the streets, among

the glass we scattered.
Not even my intention
is exact. Dust upholds
the street & I leave

a two penny penance
for the tar.
These stars, our stars,
require no motivation –

we ready for
the next dawn,
and witness
a sequence of nothing,

we hold onto the concrete,
we pull close the glass,
the shards of which matter
little, if the sun rises again.

Hasped shut by the recycling tide,
Ohio is to be a sea, land-locked
by people & their mettle.

It is not sweet to be thrummed
by madness, nor to be burned
by water, nor to be tested for purity.

This good grave has a stomach
for something bitter, but the savageness
of our repeated longing is lost waves.

AS WE REFER TO OUR BODIES

Silent little bodies
on the take, built
on falling apart,

set up overnight
in the laundry of
their revelations,

dressed like animals
& eaten by what wolf?
Still holding out,

unaccountably buoyant,
the sky is fading
like a bruise tonight,

the land & sky gone
purple & green.
The way the two of them

shape their mouths around
the end of the day
is something to behold.

Fast, thick, hot,
sometimes the bulk
of this marriage aches

like the strange way
we left, from the blossoms
of the town through

the torn fish net,
with a metaphysical
giddiness to it all

before the honey,
the honey
on our pale sheets

pooled, catching us
with such great sweet-
ness, that the tide

was ripped
from our hungry, black
memories, leaving many

people in a small town
in Ohio wondering about
who we might really be.

As we fall into
the heartquake
that is Ohio,
the earthquake
that is not,

we train our eyes
to fix upon
the ecstatic:
if you see
something, say

so.
Here, tonight,
if reality holds,
reversible, hands
in lushness touch.

Compelled by love to give
the whole thing, as whole
as a thing can get when

it is neither man nor place,
in stasis & static,
almost no words pass

between the land & the man,
& why should they?
To finish one song is enough.

On waking to the sub-vocal gulps
of hope & its mutilation,

I say, That field is boring,
but come May there will be fire,

come August; ear-high corn.

You're in a garden that
might not even exist,

the golden chill,
our soft bones

left exposed.
Seven blossoms rise to meet

the blade,
roll to the metal & grow

around it. This world
might better exist in

a discarded tire
in an abandoned playground,

the grasses grasping to
meet the true, full sun.

Once, among the plus
& the minus of belief,

I sang back to the space
between the silver
& the mirror. Here,

an eye sees clearly that
you can trust the dirt
in the garden, because

it has grown things
& you could grow

to come back, come back.

Darren C. Demaree

Already, I'm forgetting
those sounds that could be
singing. I extend my shadow

to the hulls of our ribs,
searching for the life
& light of wise wounds

that when patched poorly
become the great art, so
small in thunder-colored

lilies. Sad men begin
to vanish with the hours
that have trampled them.

Why do we, after all,
in our plain flesh &
measured fists even reach

our arms towards such
violent perfection?
Now, now too, pushing

against the road, no guts,
no wind, until the end
spells you out,

let the blood, unbound
& full of storm, flow
in spite of the burnings.

First, they found me,

then it was proven

that I wasn't there.
I was on the land,

then I was under
the thinnest ocean,

digging back & back
trying to outflank

the processional.

EMILY AS A SHEET ON THE LINE

The time is hung
time, sorrowful
only in what leaves

the tilted fabric.
If a great wind comes
& the safety pins fail,

the colors
of my beloved
will remain possible

in her state
of discovery, the last
thread, a lifeblood.

EMILY AS NOT DRUNK, BUT BY LOVE

The story is always of flight
& drowning, but I walked
past the bank of chestnuts

piled up by the animals
obsessed with symmetry,
& I was not alone

& I was not warm either
& my hands were so full of dust
that the thought of recreation

took them over. If my chest
had been a kiln I would have
reconstructed whole parts

of Emily, would have fused her
back together, would have her
in the shape of a woman,

clustered to rock, to take seasons
of me, measured, sober
& the earth, in aid, would be still.

EMILY AS A RED GINGHAM DRESS

Reel & flicker,
the row of girls
willing to wade

lining the bank
has shrunk to one.
Looks like

she was sewn in checker,
sewn in her skin
to tuck a toe

behind her heel.
When silk rushed
downstream, I was a mess.

Now, the weight
of the beam red,
plain-weave

cotton has taken
the current from the Ohio
& put it in my heart.

EMILY AS A LUMINARY

Look at the stomped paper
bags, some of the candles

in them still lit, as if
there were no feet anywhere.

EMILY AS DAWN THRIVES

The terror, true
terror of morning
is that the growing
light will shrink
back into banality
& the explosion
that first gave us
a God would ache
with nothingness
in a dark too cold
for life to fully enact
the physics of a sky
without firework.

EMILY AS A LEVELING OF GROUND

Across the snow,
the sea change of Ohio,
the axe splits wood

as an empty threat
to the whole world,
but then again, hands

can motion the life
right out of this thing.
Personally involved

in the end of the world,
what the living do,
is command the rags

& muscles to be easy
with pleasure,
to take the blanket

& pull it over all heads,
to kick legs
like an ornery child,

a knowing child
with a flat surface
to give in to an eyelid.

I found Emily,
that means I am ready
for the rest of you

to close your eyes.

EMILY AS MORE APPLAUSE

Such kick,
such wing
& belief

in the clap
of her hands.
Again

& again,
my love
is only meadow

when she allows
the sun
to rise above

the grass.
Think of death.
Now, think

of Emily
& the green
she inspires.

Darren C. Demaree

EMILY AS A HIGH WINDOW

How bird, to gloss
only for the sky, to stare
only at the blue, to find

more blue when the cloud
collides with the glass
& to never give in

to the altitude. Look up,
further up, that non-shatter
is where she is

& my reach for her flap
is dedication to the glass
& my belief that it doesn't exist.

EMILY AS THOUSANDS
OF COLLIDING BUTTERFLIES

Not as a bee, so close
to the ground, so nested
in the one, colored hive;

my love is a lunatic
with wings, a dynamo
in reds, in oranges,

with no yellow.
From a blue sky filled
with nothing

my love has taken
to darkening the sun
with the purest collision

of thundering color
& on impact,
the falling of some wing.

Follow the grasses,
you will step on the parts
of her she had no need for.

EMILY AS INNUMERABLE CIGARETTES

We needed clouds, you said,
from the stripped rib cage of a bird
on full teeter on the ceiling fan,
circling slow above the party.
Smoke up, darling, this room
needs a heaven, you said,
something that can choke out
the angels, bring them to us,
so we can parade them from lap
to lap like a girl desperate
to be the whole scene. Light all
of them at once, you said,
let the alarms turn the music
to a burning jungle, let the animals
scurry onto the street in daylight,
let them stay there to fight the blue,
let's you & me be too stubborn
to go extinct with the angels.

EMILY AS AN ANCIENT CUPOLA

Under cover
& light,
my shadow reaches

out into the night,
beyond
your hover

into the lands
stripped
of blossom.

That dance
is scary,
my legs

are defined
beneath you
& this curtain.

EMILY AS A GIRL IN A CHEMISE

Oh reach
& reach
further back

to where
those breasts
become mine

again. To where
the couch
can be our Venice

because Belle
is asleep
in her crib

upstairs. Bird,
my language

& lust, I
got those fifty
more years

you wanted
in the best art
I have ever seen.

That paint
is fresh. That paint
is drying because

of the silent animal
of our oxygen.

EMILY AS A BIRD

Amid the bees,
you are a sparrow.
Held breath,
in the shade

of this gone wind,
you can unshackle
from the fallen tree
& sprawl

into the framed moon,
past the last bloom.
If the flowers are gone,
I expect you still

to nudge the petals
on the ground,
into something pretty,

shake them out of
the weak color
of almost fall
into fall,

where the smooth sheet
of leaves & salt
will sugar us
into the un-lonely air.

Darren C. Demaree

EMILY AS UNSWERVING REALISM

Idaho, you are cold
in the field, harsh
torn trees, driving men
in two jackets to a bar
with one tap. Emily,
I know the wheat
is a metaphor, but when
my hand touches your nipple
it feels the breast around it
as well. Let this cold truth
keep me warm, even in
the unimaginable desolation.

EMILY AS A DEVOTION

Rested, the while of action,
made the whole set of wings
appear behind only one face.

BLACK & WHITE PICTURES

Tender field of human fold,
energize your ornery
with a kick, just one spinner
into Emily's gut. Let me
know that you hear the thud
of place & growing anxiety
& growing anticipation
that your legs will move
so fast we have to train
for your arrival. Don't
turn back to where you come
from, don't hold on too tight
to where you are now.
Bang your head
on the side of the wall
where my lips are resting,
rest no more in your position
on the map of my whole world.

Water, do not know
your own level.
Flood everything
with your mix
of fluids & hair
& when the town
& the people
move from the banks,
raise your tide
in victory. Water,
take me with you.
If the sun is out
too long, we will
take our salt
& become something
else, something harder
that stands
above our damages.

To lie
& say

that you will not hurt
would be

to take the sexy
out of the bee sting

& to ignore
the dying flower

that follows.
To lie & say

that I
will not break

your heart
would be

to combine
our wishes

& deny
the nature

of all fathers
& all children.

AS WE REFER TO OUR BODIES

The posing shadows
have paused in my arms.

Developing slideshow,
release the stars!

Baby, go or go ahead,
I've been dreaming

of peach trees in Ohio,
never deterred by winter

or my own ability
to touch a lighted fruit.

At the
blue of evening
my little starfish
is asleep already,
probably pissing
in the sac, floating
& flipping,
working up a good
lather of self.
I'm readying
all the towels
of my father,
preparing to clean
with the thrum
of anticipation
& almost voice.

Gone to the rug,
I've started to swim
with the blue whale
where my office
used to be. This sea
is calm and gentle
enough to go choppy
in my innards.
Rocking chair,
you are no longer
a sign of madness.

If the floors
are planked
does the curse
of the carpenter
carry over?
Wood onto
wood, my knots
will thunder
through
the burial
of the developing
self. Sapling:
fear the saw
that I might
be holding.

I am the helium bird,
rising with minimum flap

Look,
the air has nothing in it but me.
Look, the gravity is kicking in.

With no mountain & no sea,
this is still not a plain,
still not cropped & gleamed
like the balding lands
of the West or the tipping
parts of my hair. With little
lean & little to collect our waters,
I've kept my mouth open
for twenty weeks. Belle, I know
you will have an ultimate thirst.
Belle, my throat is flooded
with a young Spring. Belle,
we can be birds, & I can cool
your first screams with Ohio
& her forgiving, confused skies.

She'll dream back at me.
She'll dream of satellite instants
& zebra fish. She'll dream
of subliminal kingdoms
of arched backs & throats.
She'll dream of grown boys
& girls, drunk on their own
bodies. She'll dream of
the un-simple. She'll dream
of chickens with heads.
She'll dream of more
than eleven stars. She'll
dream of darkened roses
& their profound thorns.
She'll dream shining lines
with no context & no end.
She'll dream in orange
& mango & her lips will
quiver without knowing why.
She'll dream of dead-legged
fathers & a good creek
crinkling & smile. She'll dream
& know the collecting of dreams.

Puffy love,
the few hairs

above the button
have started to grow

over my knuckles,
like the cage

taking the bird.
My hand

has been captured
by your punching

bag. Call upon
the hold.

Call upon
your creature fear.

Kick the pressure
& kick again.

Go ahead
& go ahead

with that beautiful recklessness
of youth.

Trip, break, bleed
& then do it again, faster,

with more blood.
Hell is the high water.

Hell is a body with no scars.
Hell is a daughter that never cried

out for more of everything
& never did anything

to change the wind
her father spent his life creating.

Belle,
sit where the apple
sits. The tree
is an instrument
of death. Sit
where the apple
sits, look up
from the ground.
Extend your rot.

AS WE REFER TO OUR BODIES

How to dance with such villainy
& poise, to be in the wrong

& smile like a damned fool
& smile while you die in the fruit

of a proper damning. Belle,
your father is almost a radical.

If you can dance like him
without knowing the reasoning

you will have the proper sting
& stretch in your ankles to leave

the stage he's built around plunging
sands. Watch how fast his feet

move. Ignore what his hands do.
Each half of you that leans

to the beach will want the salted water
more than the burning granules.

No more linger to this emotional force,
every word is soaked with the coming air
of flail & sprawl & wailing need.

To appear in the door of anarchy
& love the flesh you breathe in
is to be the brightest red ball still bouncing.

AS WE REFER TO OUR BODIES

Spacious in perspective,

away from days,

lines of radiance
praise this season's treasure

& kept silver beneath the stone
walls where the apple

will try to fall.

Wintering to the core,

the sun can still whip
through to the seed

& September's non-darkness.

BLACK & WHITE PICTURE #173

Why wish you more innocence
than I was born with? Why hold
the cloud beneath the ocean?

Belle, the horrors, distanced
from you now will wait, excited
for my reach to fail you. Fear not

the deluge; maybe you'll find pleasure
in the darkness, maybe you'll dance
through the candles, avoiding none.

No matter the amount of wax
on your legs, think of the strength
in your hamstrings after the scene.

Think of the full flex of what can be
done & how pain is only an alarm
bent on putting you on whole toes.

AS WE REFER TO OUR BODIES

- The End -

Contents

DIRECTIONS FOR LEAVING   5
SECRET ANIMAL   7
THE BLIND LIMITS   8
OF A LIMITED SUGGESTION   8
THE WHEAT SANK RIPE   9
TIP OF WHISKEY   10
JOY #4   11
IMAGINING WINGS   12
KNOX COUNTY FAIR   13
WAYS YOU CAN LOSE YOUR HEART #16   14
JOY #27   15
THE SMELL OF A QUIET CITY   16
SHE PAINTS WITH NO FRAME   17

OHIOS   19
EMILY AS A SHEET ON THE LINE   40
EMILY AS NOT DRUNK, BUT BY LOVE   41
EMILY AS A RED GINGHAM DRESS   42
EMILY AS A LUMINARY   43
EMILY AS DAWN THRIVES   44
EMILY AS A LEVELING OF GROUND   45
EMILY AS MORE APPLAUSE   46
EMILY AS A HIGH WINDOW   47
EMILY AS THOUSANDS OF COLLIDING BUTTERFLIES   48
EMILY AS INNUMERABLE CIGARETTES   49
EMILY AS AN ANCIENT CUPOLA   50
EMILY AS A GIRL IN A CHEMISE   51
EMILY AS A BIRD   52
EMILY AS UNSWERVING REALISM   53
EMILY AS A DEVOTION   54

BLACK & WHITE PICTURES   57
BLACK & WHITE PICTURE #173   75

Darren C. Demaree's poems and works have appeared in the South Carolina Review, Meridian, Grain, Cottonwood, The Tribeca Poetry Review, and Whiskey Island among others. He has been twice nominated for the Pushcart Prize and deserved to win each time. He is currently writing in Columbus, Ohio where he lives with his wife and daughter.

www.ingramcontent.com/pod-product-compliance
Lightning Source LLC
Chambersburg PA
CBHW022038090426
42741CB00007B/1109